I0750324

FINISHING LINE PRESS
www.finishinglinepress.com

The Inviolable Hours

poems by

Amber Rose Crowtree

Finishing Line Press
Georgetown, Kentucky

The Inviolable Hours

~for All My Relations~

ISBN 978-1-64662-681-6 First Edition

ACKNOWLEDGMENTS

Gratitude belongs to the following publications/honors from the editors and judges who first found a home for the following poems:

North American Review, Newbury, NH Library website, and chapbook, *Harboring the Imperfect* (Dancing Girl Press, 2021), "Autumn Syndrome"
Willow Review, "All in the Binding," "The Scarce Girl," "Forever Road-Bound"
"A 1987 Photo of Female Destinies," won first adult-prize certificate of award from The Center for the Arts Literary Guild, Lake Sunapee, NH 2020 contest titled "Snapshots Through Time," final judge, Alexandria Peary. The poem is also posted on the CFA website.
The Henniker Review, "More than Audible Words," also won certificate of award and reading through Center for the Arts, Lake Sunapee, NH 2013, final judge, Ewa Chrusciel.
New England Writer's Network, "Old Flame"
The Binnacle, "The Inviolable Hours"
Birchsong II, Poetry Centered in Vermont, Blue Light Press, "How to Limb a Hawthorn Tree"
InterTown Record & Center for the Arts Lake Sunapee website: (centerforTheartsnh.org), "Ridding the Harmful"
the Aurorean, "What We are Missing"
The Briar Cliff Review, "While You Sleep, I Write:"
Covid Spring, Granite State Pandemic Poems, Hobblebush Books, "Sestina of the Isolation, 2020" (note, Mantovani reference is toward he and his orchestra's *Gypsy Soul* album, 1973.)

Publisher: Leah Huete de Maines
Editor: Christen Kincaid
Cover Art: Amber Rose Crowtree
Author Photo: Michelle Pendergrass
Cover Design: Elizabeth Maines McCleavy

Order online: www.finishinglinepress.com
also available on amazon.com

Author inquiries and mail orders:
Finishing Line Press
PO Box 1626
Georgetown, Kentucky 40324
USA

Table of Contents

I.

Autumn Syndrome

Iodized-yellow cysts,
        determined to fall,
bob in today's charcoal air
off the arms of two elderly trees.

Doomed to become pabulum,
the piebald crab apples will feed
deer, birds, ants, earth,
        maybe you or me.

The older the apple,
the sweeter its innards be.
Newborns are bitter crabs
        until they bruise sweet decay.

Humans are the opposite of apples.

Newborn, we are candied only
to slowly dissolve into bitter bald crabs,
as aged autumns would have us.

        Our bruises are never sweet.

Delivered of Gardens

Adam and Eve were born in a warm paradise,
my days started on a January abyss
at noon, as if showing up for a show-down.
While the doctor sewed my mother up,
he sang: *Mary, Mary, quite contrary, how*
do your babies grow?

This was my favorite childhood story;
how a military doctor delivered me
singing a metaphor to my mother, Mary.
I grew up learning of gardens from her—
the planting, waiting, the tending and harvest,
and the losing-of entire crops.

Did she find me cruel from the start,
holding my red, screaming, ten-pound-self
responsible for the damage done?
For I could not keep my purple cabbage leaf,
the one I had made a home out of—

will I ever have one?

All in the Binding

Kindergarten story-time, I brought my favorite book,
the large one, that fit my torso, the one
with illustrations that locked me in
like the fair lady of London Bridges, falling down;
go on, take the key, I'm fine where I am. But

in the circle of children, I could not breathe.
I could not breathe in that circle of children.

Their breath of cafeteria food distracted me
from imagining that I was *Rapunzel* and I was the
Princess bruised by the pea, and I was the
woman who guessed *Rumpelstiltskin* and I was the
women who spoke *Snakes and Pearls.*

A boy named Roman, who wished to be my prince,
grinned and gawked from the circle of children.

But he was no *Dick Whittington and His Cat,*
a boy and his cat who outsmarts men who remains
forever, a harmless illustration, a young milestone as I
grow old. Now Roman too is forever a boy, and I
am the little girl he might recall.

Claustrophobic Cure

Childhood Sundays woke me in a dark cloud—Sodom
and Gomorrah smoldering again. Opening my eyes, the day
would last twice: morning services/evening services.
Dad's aftershave, *Old Spice,* and *VO5* hairspray would waft
down the hall and collide with Mom's *Emeraude* before
I could yawn. I had the strongest sense-of-smell than anyone;

I could not breathe unless it came as ocean air or autumn leaves,
or the inhalation of apple-blossoms—anything outside of doors.

Our Dad had two selves, one in a Jack LaLanne jumpsuit
and the other, an Evangelist, starched in ironed-suit and tie.
From her hastened slippers and nightgown, Mom transformed
into clomping high-heels and dress complete with matching hat.
I knew she'd attempt to dress me for life, so I abandoned
my tights, like the bindings they were, no matter the consequence.

I could not breathe stuffed in tights, turtleneck, and patent leather shoes,
or sit for hours without fidgeting in Dad's congregation chairs.

Permission to pee became my freedom. I discovered an exit
beside the basement restrooms that opened out to a tall-grass field.
I'd peel off my turtleneck down to my slip and hide like a fawn,
inside the sweet, bendable-wall, trying not to doze off, to leave
in-time to keep my secret. Barefoot, I'd gaze into the sky, let
the sun tingle my skin back to life, and breathe...and breathe....

Our Beginning Distance

Instead of teaching me how to swim, Dad,
you showed me how deep a quarry is—
how fish do not thrive in a manmade pond,
that the banks are rock, silt, and greasy-grass; grass
that when clung-to, to fish
one's self out with, gives-way, goes limp—uproots.

Instead of showing me that I am floatable, Dad,
you sunk me like a war ship.
You taught me *anchor* not *dolphin*.
Were you testing to see if I'd float like a witch, me,
your five-year-old daughter? What then, what if
I did, Reverend? I was serious as a pupil, prepared
for mistakes. I wanted the knowledge of cartilage,
aquatic-muscle—mermaid.

Your laughing provoked other swimmers to laugh.
Trusting you was my first mistake. Where
did I go wrong in asking for your help? What
made you pick me up, whole,
and throw me in like an unwanted fish?
I cannot forget the flailing distance down,
the drinking-in through every hole
of my body, how my eyes consumed the murkiness.

I am an adult now and I'm just barely surfacing.
Many other people have tried to help undo
what you began. I've learned that I am my life-preserver;
I *can* float after all. I *can* come up for air,
staying ever-cautious of the fathom-stomach. How can I
believe you when you said,
that you were close-by the entire time? Even
if you were, how could you let me drowned just a little?

I let you baptize me at age twelve, making-believe
that you loved me enough to save; staged in front
of an audience, you fished me from the fake River Jordan.
I baptized myself that day, forgiving my fears of drowning.
It is fine to walk on water, Dad…I just want to swim.

Something More

Dad always said that my red-skinned baby forehead
looked committed by an axe to my eyes.
"That little aborigine couldn't be one of mine,"
he'd joke, and my milk-white siblings laughed.

His shortcomings never brought me tears,
only unsolved mysteries. If ever I needed him,
I found him fixing *something* of the house or vehicles,
or thumbing through his Holy Bible and taking notes
in his office in the attic of the house.

I always had to search for Mom: either
stuffed in her kitchen, resting on wicker, or hunched
over flowerbeds, realigning the perennials
or in the living room rotating the furniture, again.

Her watering cans, emptied, and abandoned in the midst
of tugged weeds (earth dried to crisp-clumps
at their roots), still comforts and cringes me—her need
to tug something with ferocity and discard it.

I dared prove myself to me, to splinter out
from that crowded house, its sullen, oval, dinner table.
In the summer, I played one-by-self basketball until
only that sphere made sense against nightfall.

My parents forbade me the challenge of teams, the skin
of my legs, sinful to eyes, *something* about unladylike;
and so, it has remained a game against myself.
How easily I can trace, across my knees, those scars
from my many fumbles.

Outskirts, Growing-In

Wild frogs bonded we siblings in that little white house tucked
on High Street, Ellsworth, Maine. The woods were our yard, a fortress
of hide-and-seek and exploring the marshes.
We handled frog eggs—the jelly-black-eyes, melting marbles—
like hospital patients, nurses, carrying newborns away from mothers.
Dad supplied five-gallon buckets and milk crates lined
with black garbage bags, secured them like a science on our mud porch.
Will they grow? I asked him. Will they survive?

The mud porch of the little white house filled quickly
with hundreds of hatching tadpoles.
We'd leave on the school bus to frog eggs in the morning
and return to colonies of swimmers. The mud porch our classroom,
we witnessed their metamorphoses; the sperm-like wriggling,
the hind legs, the front legs, the greening then
the shrinking-to-grow into fabulous, leaping, amphibians.
The day we returned the grown frogs to the pond,
my tears were not sad, but concerned, as the sound of skidders,
turning the woods under, increased the city up to our back door.

To avoid the noise-rushed world, we picnicked across the road,
where *Birdsacre* rehabilitates injured birds and human souls—
humans on the brink of forgetting the wilderness for the city-rush.
We'd walk the trails and visit the caged owls,
the one-eyed Great Horned and the one-winged Barred.
One summer, at the age of eight, I volunteered to feed the birds.
I revived songbird-beaks by-way-of syringed salt-free peanut butter;
one day I chased a seagull around the curing room to keep her calm.
Another day, while filling a kid-size swimming pool
for a Bald Eagle, my boss said: update him about Micky Mouse—I did not.
Instead, my solo words were apologies to the wild bird.
I daily consoled a flightless crow through chicken-wire, and he listened.

Today, High Street is a one-way, two-laned road, shifting tourists like fish
thru the Golden Gate to Acadia. Our empty white house looks smaller
and smaller, while *Birdsacre* clings to its own history and future.
The frogs? are alive and well; they just may take over the city....

The Scarce Girl

As if my body were an Easter egg, small,
colorful, edible, and hide-able,
            —my family could never find me.
Count to ten or call my name,
I made it clear that I wanted to disappear.

There, that's me, hiding in the nook of a tree,
Dad put me there, a challenge for us kids
to reach up high, *look-up for heaven's sake*,
            —not everything is just our height,
on this Sunday, when winter just won't let go.

Think spring, in the preparation of coloring
white eggs with the little, dry, round tablets,
whichever color is your favorite,
            —I never decided; I loved them *all*:
place a boiled egg in the wire scoop, and dip,
wait, for porous to meet dye and then,
            —magic, from ordinary to brilliant.

Notice that when you crack the colored shell
and unravel it from the boiled, sticky, plump
of baby-cheek, it has maintained the cracks
            —it won't forget the breaking, staged
like spider-webs, or tree-limb shadows cast
on snow by full moon light. Add
a little salt and pepper
            —and the whole is as good as gone.

Beyond the Nursery-Shoe

I came from you, *one, two, buckled shoe,*
a barefoot worry with a daily scratch or bruise.

"Three, four, unlock this door, *fee fie foe fum!*"
Daddy smells teenage blood…
I was the quiet one, but then, I grew…

Five, six, sometimes *sticks & stones* replaced my
bones with a *baa, baa, black sheep* without any wool.

Seven, eight, it's too late to buy a halfpenny cake;
I must bake for *Old Mother Hubbard* to keep
her from *swallowing a horse to catch the fly.*

Nine, ten, ready or not, the *old man comes rolling home.*
His dog will beg for the bone that I stole
from the dust of Hubbard's cupboard.

Hickory, dickory, dock, it's time for *Lock and Key;*
Tonight, I will dream of *Bobby Shafto* and me feasting
beneath *The Sugarplum Tree.*

II.

A 1987 Photo of Female Destinies

Mom, Me, and my little sister, frowning. Summer vacation, road-trip.
Dad had rested the 1960's *Travco* motorhome, to extend its life
on the road. While we waited for it to quit its white-steam-sighing,
he brought his camera out to capture a gigantic Arizona cactus.

My little sister and I fence Mom, as directed, and stand in front of *the star.*
Our older sister—absent—explores a Christian camp, 3,000 miles away,
where she'll meet her husband-to-be and try on Mom's Sunday shoes.

The star of the photo towers behind us, stiffly poking the desert sky
with its succulent nubs, to force the rain that just won't come.
This inside-out pincushion grows from Mom's slumped shoulders, out

of her housewife-head, as if all of the cooking & sewing she did for us
came back in one impatient clump. Her feet swell beneath the burden
in the degree of heat that melts cheese; another reason we are not smiling.

My golden-haired sister—dressed in blue—leans close to Mom's right side,
gazing at the concrete with her tiny-blue-eyes. Her three-inch feet
are firmly tucked together, readying her Air Force Sergeant future.

I am captured at eleven, a tanned, brunette, bean-pole; summer's dry gleam
a pasture in my hair. My white pants are rolled to my scuffed knees. My
white tank top hides two sore bumps, (soon-to-be trainees)—I match

Mom's scowl. This trip, she tells me that it is about time I wear a brazier.
My left-hand rests on the back of my head, my elbow forms an arrow
pointing in the direction apposing her. Deep, in the distance between us,
on my right shoulder, a highway-sign cautions, along a chain-linked fence:
Do Not Enter.

Forever Road-Bound

I'd be the only child, of the five, awake in the wee-hours,
yearning out of those black windows, watching
for signs of civilization, signs of life apart from
my family crowded for weeks in the vehicle, and observing

the back of Dad's head in front of me, at the wheel;
I wondered how much of the road ahead
he looked forward to, *the miles he'd go before he slept.*

I scouted across western deserts, northern mountains,
eastern lakes, southern terrain, and their dawn
and their moon and stars, trying to keep my hazel-eyes open,
afraid of missing a beat from the heart of the journey.

Evidence of Home

The second a cicada slits open to exit
her nymphal skin, she cannot return,
she cannot start over.
Upon emergence, her first thoughts:
freed or evicted?

It emits the sentence of Genesis 19:26
that turns Lot's wife
into a pillar of salt, her consequence
of homesickness while
watching Sodom burn, to
save *something* she has known.

How frequent the houses I have
surrendered to burning in their own
little sentences.
I cannot avoid the asymmetrical
pillar of tears. I must look back,
ask *why*—exchange my armor
for wings.

More Than Audible Words

—title inspired by Walt Whitman's, "Songs of the Rolling Earth"

Lilac-fume travels ocean waves homeward to me.
Pine-needle fingers tingle with poems, scattered
at the open and close of day; earth beds each word.

Here, deer-patience is grounded, relaxed to bound
any second with the sun, that flickering ancient flame,
beyond purple mountains; their survival each season.

I may glimpse a clan, or soloist, wearing celestial
nightgown tinsel, dreams cascading each warm exhale,
crunch of apple; breath, sweet and mammal on the air.

A Celebration of Despair

It is not the journey alone or the ozone
of spontaneous loss that has you here
releasing a scream from your throat.
No need to despair if you keep
solitary as the ever-changing moon—
unafraid of your own shadow—
and are content to circle unattached.

Grief resounds un-melted winters,
abandoned nests, and leaves the rest.
Grief does not breathe but takes breath
from the tunnels of mothers, from
the ventricles of fathers unmet. Despair
discards blue eggshells, making room
for the new or stores-away baby's clothes,
knowing they weren't meant for you.

A Road Affair

My motorcycle-man,
your astute stare, behind black rims,
separates you from the packs.
Black leather, trimmed beard, combat
wind-whippings each workday morning.
Each workday morning
you make my commute almost worth it.
Your right-hand steers, left hand props chill
on thigh; fox grin, bandana-wrapped head
cocked to one side—*loving the ride.*

My motorcycle-man,
let's never exchange names,
what we do, whom we know or knew,
where we live, places we've been & when.
Let's never argue or bring up exes, blame
each other for lost thoughts or things,
talk weather, or break each other.
Each workday morning,
let's meet, same time, same place—
cruising by at 30, opposite ways.

Old Flame

The earth wore snow
where the wild animals slept.
Evergreens changed
into Grecian robes.
My mother couldn't keep
snow away from me—I indulged;
feasted on snowballs,
slurped from ice-cycles,
sucked on ice-glazed branches.

I would trek through the woods,
and spy on our large white house—
pretending it wasn't mine.
Lying on my snow-bed, I dreamed
into blue as the sky fell white,
melting to my skin in tiny, sharp, flakes.

I would light a white candle
in a snow mound, with a match I stole
from the woodstove.
The yellow flame danced
amidst white cold silence.

Today, the sky is whitened.
Evergreens use the same dress code,
yet I'm tucked away
like a hibernating animal,
perhaps because snow is no longer sinful.

The Burning-Pile

Two elders wait in gray leaf-smoke, gazing
into a front lawn fire. One glimpse shows
they've raked their yards, cleaned their space
of winter. Someone might care, light as a leaf.

Left to themselves and memories of loves,
they rake the leaves, rake their lives—
piling layers of loves and leaves together.
Their mouths unmoved, their grey-heads down,
like funerals, like stillborns. One glimpse
mistakes them for two leaning tombstone pillars.

The elder's clothes reek of blackened leaves,
of veils they will leave behind to mulch, to ash,
where few young minds attempt to ask…
Who are your loves, who were the leaves?

The Inviolable Hours

It is not so much trying to keep alive
As trying to keep from blowing apart
From inner explosions every day.
—May Sarton, "Prisoner at a Desk"

Again, the rhythms of can't-sleep.
Three A.M., the woodstove loaded,
regardless of snow melting off

the roof, casting rain illusions.
I've added my last piece of wood,
because I am shy of kindling.

Unprepared this witching hour
in denial that winter comes and goes
as birds, in a frenzy, filled and fattened

yesterday while the sun unfroze
drinking water, exposing patches
of gravel, grass, and mud,

providing nourishment daylong.
Is it the question of provide
that sterilizes my sleep, the days

gone without, and the empty page
of tomorrow morning?
Why I avoided my woodbin?

Three A.M. provides two answers:
quiet and time—*kindling*—
to rebuild this phoenix's pyre.

Distraction through a Window, Miles from Home

—prompt of "light" from, Bob Vivian

I am looking out a window that is not mine, into
a culinary garden that is not mine. The needed-rains
have finally subsided and the herbs are gilded
with summer sun and a whispering, melancholy breeze.
Light unravels, forging negative space and shadow,
places that recall my mother's gardens. I follow
this memory-light to the eyes of my mother's cosmos;
the annual-stand of them that she plants as perennials.
They grow by their own device, though, without intention,
with little coax, without the need for attention, except by thirst.
Cosmos seeds do what they will: grow into bowing heads
or stand neck-high. Until they're top full of pollen-stars,
they *must* fall—they *must* burst and disperse, thrive
in their own universe. This noon light recalls my mother's
potted gardens, where roots grow-to-bursting out
any available hole in the pot; kick-to-crack, through plastic
or terra cotta, forcing exits back to light, free-to-roam,
free to call freedom a place, a home. I *am* like my mother,
denying I've neglected my own potted herbs and flowers
when they bust out and grow themselves—consuming
planter-pot and all—any way to get back to the earth, stretch
their legs, multiply arms, distinguish their faces, chin-up
toward the sun—all it takes is a little prompt of *light*.

How to Limb A Hawthorn Tree

—for Jordan M.

First, make sure to listen to its leaves were the July sun
becomes shade and song.
Next, know that the top limb is the mother limb and can
support your weight.
Then, scale up by harness and rope, balance
by footing the trunk.
Hope there is someone grounded to bind the loppers
to your rope and to extend the pole-saw, to hand them up.
Know which branches must go—
the greyed, the mossed, and the hollowed—
to free the tree to grow more-green,
where next spring will spur new buds.
Saw or lop the limbs and twigs with a steady rhythm,
skill and patience, dedication, is key.
Pull the propel-line to gravity back to earth
where centennial debris awaits cleanup.
Be careful of its thorns, even its berries, for hawthorns are
more human than tree thus hear every word,
feel each saw-tooth and snap.
Each time you pass by look up and never forget
that beneath where the hawthorn arcs
at its best, there once was two at labor for it.

Self-Afflictions

My rose-thorn scar defines my current
days—a stinging, pin-thin etch the length
of my triceps. Red, yet not bleeding,
in the hurry of morning duties:
to feed the pets, to warm-up my truck,
drive in the dark to clock-into work
on-time, outlast January's ice,
and somehow, keep space for my poems.

At age nine, I etched my middle name
into my arm with a safety-pin—
Rose ripened petals framed in a heart.
Why should a rose-thorn-scar hurt me now?
Roses are supposed to be asleep
to hibernate through winter's breath, yet
mine grows to my hip in the basement.
Metaphors of stress or endurance?

Ridding the Harmful

—prompt "wishbone or backbone" from, Dianalee Velie

Instead of breaking the wishbones of Thanksgiving,
I've kept them whole with wishes. I don't want to hurt anything
especially that which once connected a **Y** to wings.

In the comfort of my own despair, I honor the backbone
I seldom knew was here. From the beginning of me, it seems
someone or a group of them has wanted to crumple me like a bag
of dirty laundry. "You have to grow a backbone" some said;
no, I say, I don't: you create it for me day by day, disc by disc.
Those people would pull so greedily on a wishbone,
the magic would snuff in the snap, because they are ignorant.

Instead of breaking the wishbones of Thanksgiving,
I've kept them whole with wishes. I don't want to hurt anything,
especially that which once connected a **Y** to wings.

My vertebrae mean everything to me—no one can break me.

What We are Missing

Barred Owls are breaking,
from their barred-streaked
bosoms, a guttural hunger.
From hooked-bills, a longing

defense, a girth of breaths
hooting against the wind
to halt a mortal day—
while the boreal blue eye,

of quickening sky, unravels
in morning-glory rivulets—
the owls are ancient bards
calling off the dawn.

While we sleep-to-dreaming,
the owls are keeping nocturnal-
speech hallow, unwritten.
Their talons clench prey
in the darkness for a length

more of unmanned universe,
while the dew teardrops
their woodland-camouflage
of deep-space constellations...
Where we are uninvited, are

intruders: lackluster, ungodly.
Where we cannot fly
or breathe their body, their
system-of-words, and
stars are born and die unclaimed.

While You Sleep, I Write:

—for Greg F.

Two loons invoke the dawn over our homestead,
their falsetto wails gild the giant pine trees. Spring's
green-growth shows a lime-emerald I've never seen.
As the loons awake, the woodcocks nod-off—settling
their rounded flute-wings from pirouetting the sky
from gloaming-to-sunrise—resting their branch-like-bills.
Venus winks diamond between clouds that abscond the valley.

What took us so long to return to this home? Now we can
watch the moon discus the sky and revere the glass lakes.
Give me another word for *time* or *timing*. One that sheds
like the milk snake we found in our cabin. Mouth-to-rattle,
she had to learn patience while skinning-herself-alive,
to abandon her aged casing—renew her tender tattoos.
Perhaps it's not a word, but her metaphor I was looking for.

Sestina of The Isolation, 2020

"...It is raining today
in the mountains.
It is a warm green rain
with love
in its pockets
for spring is here,
and does not dream
of death."

—Richard Brautigan, from, "The Return of the Rivers"

Ever since losing my job, I have had the strangest dreams.
I believe my spirit is releasing toxins, like so many seeds.
This way, the hurt goes away, grows anew, cleanses like spices,
by-way-of the sunshine and the random spring rain.
Perhaps my body is morphing as I listen to more music.
My man is away nine hours a day, because he is "essential."

I was homebound this time last spring due to essential
healing from an at-work-injury. At that time, I feared music.
Every song, no matter what type, brought me tears like rain.
Unable to walk without pain, I sat determining seeds—
which ones to plant in my gardens; flowers, herbs, and spices.
I was determined to heal and shift my often-bad dreams.

I had time to renew and cultivate my future dreams
by submitting poems, and drawing again; these became essential.
I re-invoked my passion of learning medicinal herbs and spices.
During my twenties, as an herbalist-apprentice, I saved seeds,
wild and cultivated, learned by books, searched plants in the rain.
I would keep flower-heads like *love in my pockets*, like music.

These days and nights, my man and I listen to classical music
while washing the dishes or creating dinner. It is now essential
whose turn it is to sift through our vinyl records, plentiful as seeds.
We are both under age fifty, plenty of time to fulfill dreams.
Yet, with these hours in isolation, I've been using more spices,
as if I am dying—but *spring does not dream of death in warm, green, rain.*

The wood frogs, in the valley-vernal-pool, mate in the *green rain*;
early A.M. or in the gloaming, we love their vocal music.
The other day, I discovered their eggs—masses of jelly-seeds.
Where time has slowed, for me, they have hurried their dreams.

The chickadees and spring birds compose the essential.
All of this awakening, procreating, seasons poems with spices.
Ever since losing my job, I've become a kitchen-goddess. Spices,
herbs, recipes (sought or forgotten), come to me like music.
I have started my day-journal again and am writing my dreams.
I wish I had left my gruesome job sooner, to work on the essential.
Yesterday, I appeared in town for more food, wine, and seeds.
Too many folks wearing masks—erased-faces cannot smell the rain.

Today, my essential man is working from home. We shared last
night's dreams and sweet spices at breakfast. I planted seeds
before the rain returned. Tonight, we dance to music of Mantovani!

Thank you:

Leah Maines & staff at Finishing Line Press for this honor; you've answered another poet's dream. Mom, for sacrificing your writer's dream to bare and raise us. My sisters for a shared sense of humor, our key to survival. My kind, handsome, brothers for letting me borrow your pocket-knives and basketball growing up; Dad† thanks for sharing your sense of adventure on land and sea. Thank you, my grammar + high school mentors/angels: Cindy Marshall†, Pam Harmon† and others for creating extra time for my poems & art; for bringing me aside to say I have gifts to utilize. My beloved Greg, for your patience and for being my verbal-dictionary. Thank you, dear blurb writers: mentor, Richard Jackson, for taking me in at VCFA knowing I was no idler and Nicole Cooley, an ethereal-sister in poetry. Thank you, Michelle Pendergrass, my photographer, for your work and energy during our March, 5th 10° 2 ½ hour photo- shoot! I loved every minute of it; you, me, the crows, even the persistent wind.

The Inviolable Hours is dedicated, with love,
to all of you inhabiting these pages.

*

A portion of the proceeds from this book is donated by the poet to: *Birdsacre*, Stanwood Wildlife Sanctuary, (as in her poem, "Outskirts, Growing-in"). Visit: *Birdsacre* onsite: 289 High Street, Ellsworth Maine contact: PO Box 485 Ellsworth, ME, 04605, www.birdsacre.com and/or Facebook to fall in-love-with and support/volunteer at the sanctuary, for its birds-in-need, the trails, and the Pioneer Ornithologist legend herself, Cordelia "Cordie" J. Stanwood. Thank you!

Amber Rose Crowtree grew up mostly on the rocky coast of Downeast Maine. She began writing poems at age nine, romping outdoors, yet gently observing nature: not quite a "tomboy" and certainly-not your "typical female" (terms known in her childhood on how to identify and determine a female's future). At age eleven, while shooting hoops (solo) in her back yard, a rhythm of words kept repeating in her head. The vacant dog's house, next to the court, demanded to be written about, as it seemed to have weathered more quickly since her pet's recent passing away. This was the first poem that released the pent-up dam of true poetry for Amber. She set her basketball aside, found paper and pencil indoors, returned to the hardtop basketball court, and wrote a flurry of poems in tears. The tool of not-forgetting fueled her pencil that day and has ever since. At age thirteen, *The Song of Solomon*, from *The Holy Bible*, guided her in ways her parents did not intend or know; metaphor, imagery, and pastoral-sensuality, beckoned her mysterious nagging-words to continue as poetry to paper. Recollections of her childhood book, *Borrowed Black*, by Ellen Bryan Obed, illustrated by Hope Yandel, brought back Amber's first love of surreal illustrations in her kindergarten storybook (mentioned in her poem, "All in the Binding"). She later discovered other artists that speak/show, her language, such as Salvador Dali, Robert Smith of *The Cure*, Leonard Cohen, and others. Walt Whitman, Richard Brautigan, and Ray Bradbury are also her heroes, bringing her through high(hell)school. She leaped from an A.A. (Phi Theta Kappa, *Cum Laude*) at River Valley Community College, NH 2013 to earn an MFA in Writing through Vermont College of Fine Arts, 2017. Amber is a Laborer by trade, since 1995, working gardens, grounds, and buildings, enjoying physical work while keeping poetry at-heart. She still shoots hoops, and with her new (thanks to Greg) Spalding NBA Pro Tack basketball.

www.ingramcontent.com/pod-product-compliance
Lightning Source LLC
LaVergne TN
LVHW051022080826
845145LV00009B/2764
* 9 7 8 1 6 4 6 6 2 6 8 1 6 *